Kids Making
A Difference

Incredible Stories of What Kids Today
Are Doing Around the World

by
Pete Hohmann

Cover photos by Pete Hohmann
Cover design by Ashley Schermerhorn
Graphics and layout by Ted Monnin

ISBN: 1-59196-463-6
Printed in the US by InstantPublisher.com

DEDICATION

This book is dedicated to the children of Mechanicsville Christian Center. They are my friends and fellow-mobilizers. Together we are telling children around the world that kids can make a difference.

ACKNOWLEDGEMENTS

There are many people I would like to thank, especially those who contributed stories to "Kids Making a Difference." But, allow me to specifically acknowledge the following:

- Cheri Fuller, author of many books such as "When Children Pray" and "Opening Your Child's Spiritual Windows." Cheri encouraged and personally mentored me in my writing.
- Joyce Satter, a true visionary and writer who saw the unique characteristics of the Millennial Generation long before most others. Joyce shared with me many of the principles that are contained in this book.
- Jim Patterson, who has faithfully directed our Bridge Builders team for the past 12 years. Bridge Builders is our performing arts outreach team of over 100 children. Many of the quotes in this book are from members of the team and are a result of the principles Jim imparted to the children.

CONTENTS

CAN CHILDREN REALLY MAKE A DIFFERENCE?

What can a fourth grade class in a public school do to change the world? Ask Barb Vogel, a teacher at Highline Community School, in Aurora, Colorado. Her fourth grade class was studying the Civil War and the oppression of slavery. Barb shared how slavery is still a problem in North Africa today. She told of how Christian women and children in southern Sudan are stolen by Muslim slavers and taken to northern Sudan where they are sold.

WE THOUGHT SLAVERY WAS OVER

Barb said there was terror and disbelief in the eyes of her students. The kids began to cry and say, "We thought slavery was over." But, it didn't occur to the kids that there was nothing they could do. After they wiped away the tears, they said, "What are we going to do about this?" You see, while adults often listen to reports like this with their heads and think that the problem is too big or too far away, kids hear with their hearts and believe they can make a difference.

So the students wrote letters, more than 1,500 of them, to media, celebrities and public officials. They wrote to the President and First Lady, to Oprah Winfrey, Bill Cosby, and Steven Spielberg. Laura Christopher (age 11) wrote to

Colorado Senator Wayne Allard, saying, "We would like to know if you can contact the United States government and let them know what is going on, so they can take action and put a stop to slavery!"

In their letter to Hilary Clinton, the class wrote, "You once said that it takes a village to raise a child. Now we would like you to know that it takes the whole world to save the village that will raise that child."

STOP CAMPAIGN

The class formed a group called Slavery That Oppresses People, known as the STOP campaign. Through the Internet, they learned about Christian Solidarity International, a human rights group that redeems slaves, actually purchases them back and returns them to their families. It takes about $50 to $100 to redeem one slave. The kids began saving their allowances and selling lemonade, T-shirts, and old toys. The money started collecting in the old water cooler bottle located in the classroom. Soon, thanks to their own efforts and some help from some corporate donors, they had enough money to buy freedom for 150 slaves. The class made brown paper cutouts representing each slave that had been redeemed and pasted them on the classroom wall.

GREATEST ABOLITIONIST
MOVEMENT SINCE THE CIVIL WAR

Then, one of the letters hit the mark. Sumner Redstone, chairman of Viacom, responded to a letter from Barb's class and decided to put the kids and their message on his Nickelodeon Channel. News of the crusade spread everywhere, to become what is quite possibly the greatest abolitionist movement since the Civil War. To date, the class has been covered by 250 media stories, including several primetime network news interviews. Barb's children are, without a doubt, the most photographed class in the world.

The response has been incredible. A homeless man living out of his car in Alaska sent the children his last $100. A class of handicapped children raised money through a bake sale. A truck driver tells people all over the country about these kids, collects donations and has sent hundreds of dollars to the STOP campaign. Classrooms from Europe to South America are imitating what these fourth graders are doing and now nine countries are involved in the STOP campaign.

It is difficult to determine exactly how many slaves have been redeemed through the efforts of Barb's class, but it is safe to say that the number exceeds 100,000. Yet, Barb says that STOP is not a fund raising campaign. The kids themselves never asked for a penny. They just made people aware of the problem of slavery and set the example through their own efforts to make a difference.

CHILDREN SOMETIMES GET THE GREATEST RESULTS

It is incredible how kids can sometimes accomplish greater results than adults can. The three years before STOP was formed, Christian Solidarity was able to free only 1,500. Others have worked 20 years in human rights and never had the publicity given to Barb's class. Barb says, "This is God. We are fully aware we are His instruments."

Some people have questioned the wisdom of redeeming slaves through Christian Solidarity. Are we encouraging slave trade through these efforts? In order to answer this question, Barb traveled to Sudan in the fall of 1999 to see for herself how the redemption process works. The results? Barb is now convinced beyond any doubt that STOP and Christian Solidarity are doing the right thing. She called the arguments of opponents totally unsubstantiated. Just the publicity alone justifies the activity of these groups. But, what really convinced her were the tears of joy on the face of a Sudanese woman who has just been redeemed and told she is free to return to her family.

SLAVERY IN SUDAN ELIMINATED

The publicity given to Barb and her students raised awareness around the world of how slavery is still practiced today. It also opened doors for them to appear before Congress on several occasions. There was even talk in Congress that Barb's class should be nominated for the Nobel Peace Prize. Although this didn't become a reality, they did receive 14 national and international awards.

On one of their visits to Washington, D.C., Barb and her class met with then Secretary of State, Madelyn Albright. She and others in Congress pledged to do what they could to address the problem of slavery in Sudan.

In June 2000, Congress passed the Sudan Peace Act, which placed economic pressure on Sudan to stop the slavery. Included in this bill were incentives of 100 million dollars of aid a year that were only to be given to Sudan if the fighting and slavery stopped. Today, in 2004, slavery has been just about eliminated in Sudan. I am convinced this would not have happened if it were not for the kids in Barb's class.

GIVING EXTENDED TO THE LOCAL COMMUNITY

I asked Barb Vogel how her children were different today as a result of their involvement in STOP. She told me that they have extended their giving to local needs. Her students fed 45 homeless for Thanksgiving. They gave 900 canned goods to the food bank. They made flower arrangements for the elderly in a nursing home. They collected hats, mittens, and gloves for the needy. They helped feed people for Christmas. They also helped establish newly immigrated Sudanese families in the community. The class provided Christmas presents for seven new Sudanese families who had almost nothing. One child in the class even dressed like Santa Claus and distributed gifts to the Sudanese children. Barb says they cannot give enough. She says, "I've never known children to give so much."

BARB'S MESSAGE TO US

I was scheduled to speak at the National Children's Pastors' Conference the following month, so I asked Barb, "What would you want me to say to the children's workers?" Barb told me, "The voices of children ring true because they have no political or religious agenda. They just love God to love God, or love people to love people. They see a need and they want to meet it. They see suffering and they want to end it. It doesn't matter who it is happening to."

Barb continues, "God is my dearest friend, but I can't talk about this in the public school classroom, so I follow what St. Francis said, "Go preach the word of God and use words only when necessary." The kids will talk about God. They know what they are doing. This is about doing unto others what you would have them do unto you. It's all about loving God and loving your neighbor. It is pitiful that we take for granted the children that God has put on the earth for us. We don't value them or prioritize them. It's shameful."

KIDS WITH A PURPOSE

One of the reasons I have special interest in Barb's students is because I was a public school teacher for twelve years before becoming a children's pastor. I am aware that classes and even entire schools develop their own unique characteristics and personality. I wondered if Barb's class was composed mostly of gifted and talented overachievers, the kind of class that teachers with the greatest seniority and qualifications are sometimes awarded.

What Barb shared surprised me. She said, "I didn't get the bright ones. I had the most learning disabilities impacted class last year in the fourth and fifth grade. Yet, my class has never been beat in the Iowa basics. They outscored everybody! It's because they have a purpose. Helping others has become a priority and they have found such joy in giving to others."

Barb says, "God is mobilizing kids today because they are listening. They will listen to God. They will come unto God. They have no ulterior motives. Isn't it wonderful that it is children? Doesn't it make sense? The Bible says for us to come unto God as a child."

Barb's original students are growing up, but she meets with them once a month. Their involvement did not stop just because slavery in Sudan has been almost eliminated. Now they are helping former slaves adapt to their newfound freedom.

KIDS MAKING A DIFFERENCE

In the following chapters you will read more stories like the one of Barb's fourth graders. Some of these stories will tell about children making a difference through prayer and through sharing their faith in Jesus Christ. In other stories you will see children making an impact in their churches, in their communities, and in issues that have worldwide influence. You will also see how the present generation of children is a generation of destiny, designed by God to accomplish His greatest purposes. We will refer to them as the "Millennial Generation," those born in the last 20 years. The Millennials may be the most important generation that has ever lived. But, if that is true, we are the most strategic generation because it is our responsibility to train and equip them to fulfill their destiny.

Each chapter will also include a "Next Step Readings." This will include recommended books, web sites, and free articles and handouts from presentations at national conferences that you can receive upon request from the author of this book.

NEXT STEP READINGS:

✶ www.iabolish.com has good information on STOP, including ways that you can be directly involved.

✶ "Dream Freedom," by Sonia Levitin, is a novel based on a true story and real-life contemporary events concerning the life of a teenage girl in Sudan. It is for ages 10 and up and is available through Silver Whistle Harcourt Inc.. Log onto www.harcourtbooks.com and enter "Dream Freedom" into the search box.

KIDS MAKING A DIFFERENCE THROUGH PRAYER

HOPE FOR MONGOLIA

Far-reaching events were being set in motion by God as a nine-year-old girl selected Mongolia to be the topic of her report for a home school assignment. One of the sources of information was an article about Mongolia she found in "Mountain Movers" magazine. This monthly publication was the official foreign missions magazine for the Assemblies of God, and it often contained articles on peoples and countries that had no strong Christian church. The article she used for her report described how there were very few believers in all of Mongolia. She read about how Mongolians sometimes placed Buddhist altars in the felt tents where they lived.

This nine-year-old was so burdened for Mongolia that she prayed for two years that God would replace the Buddhist altars in their felt tents with Bibles. After two years of intercession, she saw the words "Hope for Mongolia" on the cover of a recent issue of Mountain Movers Magazine. The "Hope for Mongolia" article described a revival in Mongolia where 500 people had come to Christ. She knew this article was God's way of telling her He had answered her prayer. You see, this girl's name is Hope, Hope Smith. She said, "That day, I learned there was another 'Hope' for Mongolia."

During the following year these 500 Mongolian believers

grew to 1,000 and have started a church. Can you guess its name? "Hope Assembly," of course. As many as 2,000 have attended services at Hope Assembly and they have even pioneered another church. Several years later, two Christian orphanages were started in Mongolia with the names H.O.P.E. #1 and H.O.P.E. #2, each with about 15 children. H.O.P.E stands for "Homes of Peace Enterprises." Amazing! I doubt whether all the use of the word "Hope" is a coincidence!

HOPE BECOMES A MISSIONS MOBILIZER

Shortly after this, Hope gave her testimony in children's church at Mechanicsville Christian Center. She shared how she knew God had answered her prayer through the title of the article. I had never written to our headquarters before, but I decided to write up her story and send it to the Department of Foreign Missions. They recognized her intercessory role regarding the revival in Mongolia and they published an article about Hope Smith in Mountain Movers, the same magazine where she saw the other two articles about Mongolia.

Before the magazine was printed, however, Joyce Booze, the editor of "Mountain Movers," called me and said that I had forgotten to include Hope's last name in the article I sent. I believe I was out of the country and unavailable when she called. Joyce was pressed for time and had to send the article on to the printer with a fictitious last name, hoping to change it later if time permitted. She inserted the name "Smith," not knowing it was Hope's real last name. This just served as further confirmation to me that God really did use Hope Smith to stand as an intercessor for a nation.

Later that year Hope's story was also published in the World Edition of the "Pentecostal Evangel," which is the official magazine of the Assemblies of God Movement around the world. Such interest was generated in her story that the Assemblies of God decided to feature her in a segment of their video magazine called "Mandate." They sent someone to our church from headquarters to tape Hope.

BRIDGE BUILDERS OUTREACH
TEAM RECOGNIZED

In the course of my conversations with headquarters, I shared with them that our church also had an outreach team composed of children, called Bridge Builders. At the time, Bridge Builders consisted of about 50 children with an average age of about 11. They minister in the community through the performing arts and practical service projects. The Department of Foreign Missions decided to include Bridge Builders in the "Mandate" video magazine, along with Hope's story.

The articles and video generated many calls to headquarters from people wanting to know how to involve their children in missions and outreach. In order to respond to these requests for information, I was asked to conduct workshops at our national missions conferences and to write a book called "Mobilizing Kids for Outreach." I was also asked to produce a video called "Mobilizing Kids for Ministry."

THE GREAT COMMISSIONARY KIDS

While all this was happening, Sandy Askew was the national director of Boys' and Girls' Missionary Crusade (BGMC), which is the missions education program for children in the Assemblies of God. But Sandy's vision extended beyond the children of her denomination. In the late 90's, about the time when Hope's story was really circulating, the doors were finally opened for Sandy to start a new daughter ministry called The Great Commissionary Kids. This ministry is dedicated to involving kids in missions and outreach in all denominations. Although Sandy had the Great Commissionary Kids concept in her heart for many years, no one would question that Hope made a contribution towards its birth and development.

Through the faithfulness of a nine-year-old girl praying for Mongolia, doors were opened for people to hear about how God is using kids to make a difference today. Hope actually impacted two nations; Mongolia by her intercession and America through her missions mobilizing. Isn't it just like God to use the small and weak to contribute to great movements?

CHILDREN WANT TO PRAY

Within every child God has placed a desire to pray. According to Esther Ilnisky, founder and director of The Global Children's Prayer Network," it is the responsibility of parents and children's workers to release and mentor children to pray. To "release" means to "set free from restraint." For a child, restraints may include fear or just not knowing what to pray. Children tend to be egocentric in their prayers, but not selfish. Egocentric means their world is small. Their prayers are limited to pets, family and friends. It is our job to enlarge their world and also mentor children how to pray. Without this coaching, the prayers of children remain the typical bedtime prayers that never change until eventually, the desire itself to pray is lost.

THE MOST EFFECTIVE PRAYER

When children are properly coached, they can be even more effective than adults when they pray and intercede for others. In her book, "When Children Pray," Cheri Fuller makes the following observation: "Kids have not yet learned the caution and cynicism that too often accompanies adulthood, most children naturally possess 'big faith.' I believe that it is their wide-eyed wonder, openness, and expectation that Jesus found so endearing, that prompted Him to say that all of us should maintain those childlike qualities in our prayer lives with Him."

I have observed that the children's prayers are usually simple, honest, and straight to the point. Their prayers are full of faith and seem to zing right to the heart of God. Most kids don't compose their prayers for the benefit of those who are listening.

WORLD SHAPERS

Esther Network International (ENI) is devoted to mobilizing kids around the world for intercession. Esther Ilnisky, founder and director of Esther Network, says that nearly two billion children, ages twelve and under, are on earth today. Her vision is to have millions of them join forces with ENI Children's Global Prayer Movement to pray for all the children of the world. These kids are called "world shapers."

Esther developed several "prayer tools" to help children intercede. Her book, "Let the Children Pray," describes these prayer tools and also how your kids can become world shapers through Esther Network International.

In this book, Esther writes, "Children have a very active role in ENI simultaneous global prayer gatherings. They pray — and pray — and pray! They don't ask for snacks, toys, games or even videos! They stay amazingly focused. Their anointed intercession is a constant proof of God's sovereign work in and through them. Some of their most powerful prayers have occurred after several hours of intercession."

PRAYER MEETINGS AND PRAYER WALKS

At Mechanicsville Christian Center, children are given many opportunities to pray. There is a monthly prayer club that meets on Sunday afternoon. We have also conducted many prayer walks for children throughout the city. Usually about three sites, such as the observatory deck on city hall, are selected for the prayer walk. We have also conducted prayer watches where children prayed through the night using a variety of activities to keep them focused. During a week of camp, we conducted

24/7 prayer. The children took turns praying around the clock for needs in their community and around the world for one week!

MENTAL PICTURES

God often speaks to children through pictures in their minds during times of prayer. For example, on one prayer walk the children were interceding at St. John's Church, which is where Patrick Henry gave his famous "Give me liberty or give me death" speech. A young child drew a picture of the church grounds all planted up like a vegetable garden. In the drawing, God was gathering in the ripe fruit and vegetables. The girl believed God gave her this picture in order to show the kids that there was going to be a great harvest of souls in Richmond. That picture energized the children's prayers for revival. A wave of revival that touched over a hundred churches did come to Richmond the following year.

THINGS ONLY GOD WOULD KNOW

It is amazing how God will direct children regarding what to pray. At a Global Harvest National Prayer Conference, eleven year-old Amanda was approached by an older woman who needed prayer. Amanda asked for specifics, but the woman said, "You ask the Lord what I need." Amanda began to pray for direction from the Lord for her prayer. Suddenly, without any background information, Amanda said," You are from South America, and you have been hurt by your ex-pastor. You must forgive him in order for you to be set free". The older lady fell to the ground and began crying out, "Lord forgive me, forgive me, what have I done? I will go to Brazil and ask for forgiveness!"

DEPENDENT ON ADULTS

Children have a tremendous capacity to make a difference

through their prayer. But, they are totally dependent on us to equip them to pray. The desire is within them, just waiting for us to release and mentor it. Please investigate the following "Next Step Readings" to show you how.

NEXT STEP READINGS:

✶ "Let the Children Pray," by Esther Ilnisky, Regal Press
✶ For resources and prayer tools from the Children's Global Prayer Movement log onto www.cgpm.org
✶ "When Children Pray," by Cheri Fuller. Also check out Cheri's web site at www.cherifuller.com for prayer articles and resources.
✶ Free handout from Pete Hohmann's "Leading Children in Prayer" workshop presented at the 2001 National Children's Pastors' Conference. Request at petehohmann@cs.com (sent as a Microsoft Word Attachment).

KIDS MAKING A DIFFERENCE THROUGH SHARING THEIR FAITH

MONICA TORO IN COLUMBIA

The world is full of stories of kids making a difference like Hope Smith. Let's shift our focus to a child in South America. Her name is Monica Jasmin Toro. At the time of this story she was ten years old and from one of the poorest barrios in Bogota, Columbia. It should be noted that South America is not a place where the ability of children to minister is widely recognized, especially if you also happen to be a young girl. But, once again, God seems to delight in moving in the most unexpected ways.

The church Monica and her family attended, Iglesia Cruzada Cristiana de Santa Isabel, was teaching the Evangelism Explosion method of witnessing to their congregation. Evangelism Explosion International helps equip believers to share their faith through diagnostic questions, simple statements, illustrations, and Scripture.

WHY NOT TEACH CHILDREN TO SHARE THEIR FAITH?

A children's worker at the church pondered, "Why can't we adapt this training to children and teach our kids to share their faith?" An experimental Kid's Evangelism Explosion was launched and Monica was among the children who were trained.

Because there were no schools in her immediate area, Monica had to ride a public bus, two hours each way, to school each day. She would sing Bible choruses out loud while on the bus. After a few weeks of singing, one of the passengers asked where the words of the choruses came from. She said, "The Bible." She then recited the Bible verses from the choruses.

Following this pattern for the next few weeks, the passengers became well acquainted with Monica. Then one day, she began asking her fellow passengers the Evangelism Explosion questions. The first one goes, "If you were to die tonight, do you know for sure that you would go to heaven?" The second question, which further ascertains the true spiritual state of a person, goes like this: "If God were to ask you, 'Why should I let you into heaven?' what would you say?" Through these questions Monica found opportunity to share the Gospel through what she had learned in the Evangelism Explosion training. That day, ten people, including the bus driver, wanted to accept Christ as Savior. The bus driver stopped the bus and all made professions of faith in Christ.

A CHURCH IS PLANTED THROUGH A CHILD

Monica then invited the people who had accepted Christ to her house where her parents led them in Bible study. After a month, 30 people were arriving at Monica's house for Bible study. After their pastor visited the Bible study, he made arrangements for an assistant pastor to work with these new Christians. One year later, the group became a daughter church with over 130 people attending on Sunday — all because a ten-year-old was obedient to share her faith.

KID'S EVANGELISM EXPLOSION IS BORN

Inspired through Monica's example, Evangelism Explosion International has developed a program for equipping kids in grades two through six to share their faith in Christ. Our church hosted a Kid's Evangelism Explosion Workshop and we have seen the fruit. Not only have our children learned to share their faith more confidently and effectively, but they are now able to discern who is truly a believer and who is not.

For example, Hunter (age 7) was participating in an outreach at a park in a poor urban area. He said, "At the park I got to witness to three boys. At first they claimed to be Christians, but after using the Kids EE tract, I found that they didn't know Christ and after talking to them about Christ they accepted Christ."

Evangelism Explosion for Kids represents one more movement where kids are making a difference. Just like God used Hope Smith to contribute to the Great Commissionary Kids, He also used Monica to help birth Kid's Evangelism Explosion.

KID'S SPEAKING OUT

Can kids really make a difference by sharing their faith with others? Elisha, who started sharing her faith at 10 years old, thinks so. As she reflects back over 6 years of leading others to Christ she shares, "God has shown me that the lost people are not just numbers. They are real people. Now I have names and faces of the lost that have come to know God. Being able to lead someone to Christ, to see their faces light up when I tell them that there is a Savior that loves them is the greatest joy of my life."

Some, like Ashley who is 12, have even felt a call to be an evangelist. "He gave me more boldness to go out and witness for Him. I don't care what other people think. In Bridge Builders (our outreach team composed of children) God told me He wants me to be an evangelist."

Children like Katie, age 11, have learned to look beyond the outside to the needs within. "I learned that you can't judge a book by its cover. Some people may look really sinful on the

19

outside, but really on the inside they are in pain and seeking for something or someone to turn to."

Josh, age 11, reflects back on an outreach in an apartment complex in the inner city. "The kids were so playful. They loved having us around and they followed us wherever we went. I met a kid named Jamil. He was hungry for God and he gave his heart to Jesus. When we where leaving, he asked, 'Are you coming back and is Jesus going with you?' I said we were going but Jesus will stay right in your heart, and I prayed [for him] right there."

KIDS ARE EFFECTIVE EVANGELISTS

Yes, kids can effectively share the gospel and lead people to Christ. In fact, no one is more effective at leading a child to Christ than another child who has been trained to share his or her faith. Even though a gospel presentation by a child may lack all the components and the order that we think are necessary, the Holy Spirit somehow uses it and the message is understood.

David Walters, author of "Equipping Younger Saints," writes, "Even though they may be young, immature and inexperienced, God's Holy Spirit working in them IS the power of God." Kids are also effective in witnessing to adults because they do not have the same inhibitions as adults. They have boldness in sharing and a contagious enthusiasm. They are usually more faithful to obey the Holy Spirit's promptings than adults. They do not have the barriers that adults often have developed. As adults, it is our fear of rejection, not the lack of Biblical knowledge, that keeps us from sharing our faith.

I also believe that God simply anoints kids to share their faith because they are more likely to depend on Him. Anointing is simply power — power to serve. The Bible tells us to be like a child if we want to be used by God — they ARE children. In all their fear, insecurities, and weakness, they simply call out to God for help. And, He hears and answers their prayer of innocent faith.

FRIENDSHIP EVANGELISM

Kids often share their faith through simple friendships, which seem to come easier to them than for adults. Bethany, a ten year-old from Trinity Presbyterian Church in Jackson, Mississippi writes, "It was a bright, sunny day. I had run outside to play in the creek, when to my surprise, I found a Chinese girl there already. I introduced myself, and soon the two of us were swinging high into the air on our swing-set. Then I invited Melissa to a week long Vacation Bible School at our church. The week was full of fun songs, Bible memory, crafts and games. Later I asked Melissa to a missions conference at the church. During prayer time, Melissa gave her heart to the Lord. Seeing Melissa come to Christ made me want to do it all over again with another boy or girl."

KIDS MUST BE TRAINED TO SHARE THEIR FAITH

Once again we see that kids have a tremendous capacity to make a difference. But, we also see that they are totally dependent on adults to equip them to share their faith. A child must be taught to ask the right questions so they can discern who is a believer and who is not. Sharing the gospel is a combination of content and persuasion. Therefore, kids must know how to effectively communicate the message of salvation and they must be able to persuade others to place their trust in Jesus for eternal life.

Neglecting to equip our children to share their faith is no longer an option. In his book, "Kids in Combat," David Walter writes, "Militant Marxism and Islam is being taught to kids around the world while our kids are only allowed to play. Satan is preparing an army but the church is entertaining her children."

‿‿‿ is preparing His own army, but they will be motivated by love, not hate. I am convinced that the ultimate solution to terrorism will not be through politics or military might. The only lasting solution is the Good News of the Lord Jesus Christ shared in love and in the power of the Holy Spirit.

Equip your children to share their faith. It will not only advance the Kingdom of God, but it will strengthen their own faith by causing them to examine and articulate what they believe. Our beliefs are never fully integrated into our own lives until we share them with others.

NEXT STEP READINGS

✶ Kids Evangelism Explosion is at www.kidsee.org or contact Dr. Karen Gushta at Kid's Evangelism Explosion International, P.O. Box 23820, Fort Lauderdale, FL 33307, telephone 954-491-6100 ext. 315.

✶ "Kids in Combat," by David Walters (Good News Fellowship Publishing). This book has a Pentecostal perspective, but is useful reading for any denomination. David's web site is www.goodnews.netministries.org

✶ Free handout from Pete Hohmann's "Equipping Kids to Share Their Faith" workshop presented at the 2002 National Children's Pastors' Conference. Request at petehohmann@cs.com (sent as a Microsoft Word attachment).

KIDS MAKING A DIFFERENCE THROUGH MINISTRY IN THE CHURCH

Pastor Bob can't figure out why there are not more adults in his church involved in ministry. Most of his members have been raised in the church. You would think that they would understand the importance of service. Why do they just sit there in the pews, so unmotivated to get involved no matter how many sermons Pastor Bob preaches on serving? To find one possible reason why so many don't actively serve, let's visit the children's church.

John, the children's church director, has 50 children sitting before him, a good number of which are chattering loudly as children typically do as they wait for something to begin. John and his staff love ministering to the kids, and they are quite skilled at drama, puppets and object lessons. John even sings well and plays the guitar. It's time to begin. John opens the children's service saying, "Kids, we've got a great program here for you today. We want you to sit still, be quiet, and listen as we minister to you. We have "quiet seat prizes" for those who stay in their seats, listen, and don't disturb the other kids."

TRAIN UP A CHILD

As usual, the adult workers do a great job of ministering to the kids. Today Suzie receives a prize at the end of children's church because she sat quietly, didn't hit any of the children next to her, and paid attention to all the adult workers as they ministered. If only we could clone Suzie! Of course, Tommy didn't do so well. He's the hyperactive-attention deficit child. He is failing in traditional public school education and isn't doing much better in church programs either. He didn't receive a prize today because he kept talking and interrupting the adults while they were ministering.

Let's get back to Pastor Bob's adult congregation in the main service. The adults are quietly sitting still and listening to Pastor Bob minister, but the sad reality is that the majority are not involved in active ministry or mission. Could it be that they are only doing what they were taught to do as children? After all, they are only fulfilling the Biblical principle, "Train up a child in the way he should go, and when he is old, he will not depart from it." If we train up children to believe that quietly sitting and listening while someone else ministers to them fulfills their Christian responsibility, then it will be difficult to change that attitude as an adult. About, 85% of our attitudes are formed in childhood. Pastor Bob only has 15% of attitude left to mold with his adult congregation.

CHILDREN MUST BE EQUIPPED TO MINISTER

I don't want to criticize the children's church staff in our illustration too much. Self-control is very important for children to learn and in many situations, a traditional, adult-centered children's church program is probably the most viable way to minister to a large group of children. We even reward children for self-control in our own children's church. But, somewhere in our discipleship of children, they must be equipped to minister instead of adults just ministering to them. Kids need to be given opportunities to make a difference in the lives of others.

Let's go back to the two children referred to in children's church. Suzie, our quiet girl, may very well be the one that we never hear from again. If children are not equipped to minister to others, many kids like Suzie slip away from the Lord after they leave the insulated church setting of their childhood. But, what about hyperactive Tommy who can't keep quiet or sit still? Tommy will probably be your next pastor, especially if he is given an opportunity to minister to others as a child.

Fortunately, not every church is like Pastor Bob's. Our story in this chapter is not about an individual child, or even a classroom of children, but rather a church full of children. What is the difference in this church? At Mechanicsville Christian Center the kids do the ministry. It is here that I have the privilege of being the children's pastor.

WELCOME TO KIDS CHURCH

Let's say you are fairly new to the church and your somewhat shy child is finally willing to check out KIDS Church, which is the worship service for grades 1-5. We should say here that "KIDS" in KIDS Church stands for Kids In Divine Service (adapted from the Charisma Life KIDS Church curriculum). As you enter the meeting room your family is greeted by three children at the registration table. These kids are a few of the 20 children who serve as Junior Leaders in KIDS Church. After receiving a nametag, a Junior Staff Leader is assigned to "be a friend" to your child and ease the transition into this new experience.

The worship in KIDS Church consists of the familiar worship songs from popular CD sound tracks, but the worship leader is a 10 year-old girl named Cassidy. About 7 other boys and girls are helping her on the worship team, some singing with microphones, others leading in creative movement. Josh, a 14 year-old, is running the sound. A puppet skit is part of the lesson. Their leader, Philip, is 15 years old and the puppeteers are all 12 or younger. The puppet team is just one of the many KIDS Clubs at Mechanicsville Christian Center.

Like many of the clubs at the church, the puppet team practices once a month on Sunday afternoon. The Drama Club, which is led by a 14 year-old girl named Libbey, performs the drama that reinforces today's lesson. At a time of prayer around the altar, children are praying for children, without being prompted by an adult. As parents come to pick up their children at the conclusion of the service, they are given the weekly take-home sheet by a Junior Leader. Later that week, your child receives a call from one of the Junior Staff Leaders welcoming him or her to KIDS Church.

GOD'S GARDEN

Down the hall is God's Garden, the Preschool and Kindergarten children's church. As expected, there is a Bible story and worship, but in God's Garden, the 75 preschoolers spend the majority of their time working at 10-12 learning centers. Every learning center has an activity that reinforces the Bible story for the day. The children move from center to center as they desire. Seats or mats determine how many children can stay at a center.

Each learning center has a "task card," which consists of typed instructions describing how the worker should interact with the preschoolers. For example, one Sunday the lessson may be the story of creation from Genesis. One learning center would have preschoolers coloring pictures of animals with crayons. The task card instructs the worker to talk to the preschoolers about their favorite animals and how God created all the animals. The focus is relationship, however. At this age, relationship is more important than curriculum and attitudes are formed, including how the child feels about God and the church.

It takes about 50 workers to staff this preschool children's church. Some serve once a month, others twice a month. The primary directors are there every week so that there is a continuity of relationship, which is important to preschoolers. But, what is unusual about God's Garden is that half the staff is composed of preteens and teens. This has been working well for over ten years.

Down another hall a group is meeting called "God's Special Music," which is a Sunday School class for disabled children, such as those with autism. It's rare to find a ministry like this in a local church, but what is even more rare is to see all the preteen and teen kids working with these disabled children. Their training is rigorous and the demands are great, but they desire to serve.

KIDS CLUBS

There are many KIDS Clubs at Mechanicsville Christian Center. Generally they meet once a month for training. Their purpose is to equip children for ministry and disciple them through the teachable moments "doing ministry together" provides. For example, the Sound Club not only learns how to set up and run sound systems, but they also do a Bible study together. This past fall, the Practical Service Club learned about compassion as they raked leaves for some of the church's elderly shut-ins. Last Sunday afternoon the KIDS Prayer Club learned more prayer principles as they interceded for the church.

KID-2-KID

KIDS Clubs partner with me in ministry at Mechanicsville Christian Center, but how can I possibly take care of the over 350 children who attend the church? I have heard that one pastor cannot personally care for more than about a hundred people. But, I have over 350 children under my care, plus their parents, plus I carry all the general responsibilities of being an associate pastor such as preaching, counseling, weddings, and funerals.

Ephesians 4 has been my guide here. This verse tells me

that my job as a pastor is not to DO all the ministry, but rather to equip the saints to do the work of the ministry. I believe that any child who has accepted Christ is a "saint" and therefore can be equipped for ministry. But, can these children be equipped to care for one another?

KID-2-KID is a ministry in our church where older children care for younger ones. An older child who is a KID-2-KID leader (5th grade or older) is assigned about five younger children. The KID-2-KID leader must call each of their younger children at least once a month to see how they are doing. They are also encouraged to pray for them and also to spend some personal time with them. Once a month the KID-2-KID leaders have a meeting and we talk about how things are going and how we can better minister to the children in our group. In addition, the leaders turn in a report that alerts me of any special concerns that require my personal attention.

LINKING THE GENERATIONS

In all the ministries I have shared, older children and teens can be seen ministering to younger children. Everyone is the winner in this arrangement. The preteens are benefiting by being trained and released to ministry. The church is benefiting because good preteen workers are filling needed positions. But, more importantly, the younger children are benefiting as a result of learning from the experiences of the older children.

There is great blessing when older children minister to the younger ones. Normally ministries in churches are very age specific, basically following the same model as the public school. Kids are isolated by age groups. Younger children are not usually given the opportunity to learn from the experiences of the older children. But, I believe the biblical model calls for a "linking of the generations."

When we "link the generations" in the church, the adults mentor the teens, the teens mentor the preteens, and the preteens mentor the younger children. Of course, teens often minister to preschoolers and adults to preteens. But, when you observe the intergenerational ministries, kids definitely emulate the age group immediately above them. I know that a preteen usually has greater influence on an 8 year-old than an adult. This benefit of linking the generations is not usually seen in a church, however, because the older children have not been trained and released to minister.

There are even more benefits of linking the generations in the church. When we equip the older kids to minister to the younger in the church, it gives the older kids a sense of purpose. Compassion and concern for the younger kids develop as they invest their lives in the younger children. At first preteens may not want to spend time with the "little kids." But, as the preteens begin to take ownership of ministry, they begin to develop a sense of responsibility for those younger than themselves. The older kids learn how to be "servant leaders" to the younger children instead of bosses or bullies.

LET KIDS BE THE CHURCH

In an article in the September/October 1999 issue of "Children's Ministry" magazine entitled "Let Kids Be the Church," Paul Allen, editor of "Vital Ministry Magazine," makes some challenging statements regarding our traditional approach to children's ministry. He says, "Let's quit doing church to kids and invite them into being the church of God. A healthy church is where ALL the members work together."

Allen further states, "It's time for us to move beyond just preparing them for ministry tomorrow; we must prepare them for ministry today. Fortunately most churches have moved beyond the child-care-only level. Yet it is time for us to move from creating spectator Christians to releasing participating Christians."

But, are kids today willing to make the kind of commitment

...stry in the church will require? Look around you at ...e incredible commitments kids make to sports or other activities. Millennial children want to be committed to a team, an ideal, or a cause. Therefore, the real question is, "Who is going to get their commitment?" We said earlier that people don't resent being asked for great commitment if there is a great purpose behind it. What greater commitment is there than advancing the Kingdom of God through the local church?

LOOKING INTO THEIR EYES

In the "Let Kids Be the Church" article, Allen also writes, "'How many eyes did you see today?' Spend time looking into their eyes and listening to their hearts. As you worship, note those who easily enter into praise. Notice the ones that rise to the occasion as leaders. Observe children with mercy and grace toward others. Identify kids with artistic ability. Keep a notepad handy to record the strengths and abilities you recognize in each child."

I encourage all my Sunday School teachers to do this. For example, if a child is musical, why not give that child the assignment of finding a song that reinforces the upcoming lesson? Or, the artistic student could draw a picture that illustrates the lesson. For every gift, there is a way that child can contribute to the class. Your job is to equip and release those children to use their gifts in the church.

MOTIVATIONAL GIFTS

Helping children identify their motivational gifts is a great tool for equipping them to minister in the church. Motivational gifts are our God-given abilities — the way God designed us so we can minister to others. In our church we utilize the Spiritual Gifts Questionnaire and the "Discovering Your Children's Gifts" book, both by Don and Katie Fortune. There are several questionnaires designed for each age group, from preschool through teen. The questionnaire is based on Romans 12:1-2, and it identifies strengths in seven areas: Perceiver, exhorter, administrator, teacher, compassion, giver, and server.

Every year I conduct a children's retreat at our church, and every fourth year our retreat theme is the motivational gifts. The children take the Spiritual Gifts inventory, with the help of their parents, before arriving. All weekend we conduct activities that help the children understand the gifts.

RETREATS FOR TRAINING

Regardless of the theme of our children's retreats, ALL retreats include ministry training workshops. These workshops usually last two hours and they train children in skills such as drama, puppets, choreography, preaching, setting up and running sound systems, and leading worship. On the Sunday morning of the retreat, we conduct a service where the children do most of the ministry. For example, the children from the preaching workshop do a "tag-team" sermon. Children also lead worship, perform drama and puppet skits, and run the sound system. Everyone gets a chance to demonstrate his or her ministry skill.

We have also followed this pattern in our Kid's Camp each summer, including ministry training workshops each day. We culminate the week at camp with each of the groups demonstrating what they learned. In both the retreats and camps, the children are given a safe and controlled environment where they can take their first steps of ministering to others.

PICK A PLACE TO START

It took many years to develop the children's ministries at our church. But, no matter what your position, there is a place you can start. Possibly you could minister in your church as a family. If you are a children's worker, use one of the ministries

...ve shared as a springboard to developing your own ideas. The important thing is to start somewhere, or we may be found guilty of raising the next generation of spectator Christians. Or worse, we may be responsible for our children becoming bored with their Christianity. Children who are not given opportunities to minister in the church often develop a "whatever" attitude about Christianity by the time they reach their preteen years. So, do you want your kids to be excited about being a Christian? Equip them and release them to minister in the church.

NEXT STEP READINGS

✶ "Discovering Your Children's Gifts," by Don and Katie Fortune (Chosen Books) is a great resource. Katie has also developed gift inventories for all ages. For more information www.heart2heart.org, or email fortune@heart2heart.org, or call 360-297-8878 to place an order.

✶ "Equipping Younger Saints," by David Walters (Good News Fellowship Publishing). This book has a Pentecostal perspective, but it is useful for any denomination. David's web site is www.goodnews.netministries.org

✶ "Children's Ministry" magazine has a web site which includes ideas and information on equipping children to minister in the church. Log onto www.cmmag.com or call (760) 738-0086 for subscription information.

✶ Free handout from Pete Hohmann's "Equipping Kids for Ministry in the Church" workshop presented at the 2003 National Children's Pastors' Conference. Request at petehohmann@cs.com (sent as a Microsoft Word attachment).

KIDS MAKING A DIFFERENCE
IN THEIR COMMUNITIES

In this chapter you will see children making a difference in their communities through reaching out to others in a nursing home in Omaha, a city park in Chicago, a small rural community in South Carolina, and even at a basketball court in inner-city Philadelphia.

GRAND FRIENDS

The ministry is called "Grand Friends," and it pairs kids who are 12-18 years old with nursing home residents. Debbie Tesarek, who directs the Grand Friends ministry, started ministering in nursing homes 10 years ago. Debbie shares, "I would take my children with me to the nursing home hoping to model Jesus' love to my children and the residents. About six years ago I began bringing the youth of my church to the nursing home. My vision was to create a wider awareness of the men and women living and dying in the care centers of our land. I wanted to guide and challenge the youth to be Jesus to these people who He loves and cares for so deeply."

Debbie and the kids in Grand Friends adopted a specific nursing home, a place they describe as one of the most needy homes in the city. The kids visit their Grand Friends in this nursing home for 30 minutes at least once a month. They usually spend the first 10 minutes playing games with their

33

Grand Friend such checkers or cards. The remaining 20 minutes is devoted to conversation.

Debbie teaches the kids the art of conversation and the children learn to ask their Grand Friends questions such as, "What made you the happiest in life?" Or, "If you could give me any advice to make my life full, what would it be?" The kids also learn to seek out the interests of the residents. Most importantly, they have learned the importance of just being a friend and loving the residents to God. The kids are committed to their Grand Friends for the remainder of their Grand Friends' lives.

The following is a story from one of the kids and her grand friend. I have changed the name of the Grand Friend to avoid offending any family members.

"JESUS MUST HAVE SENT YOU"

Elisha, age 15, had a Grand Friend named Jack who she visited for two years. Elisha shares, "I was so frightened the first time I saw Jack. He was a big man confined to a wheelchair. I was afraid he would reject me or he would be mean. As I continued to come, I came to love his voice. Jack told me he was close to his children and that he missed them. He said they didn't come to see him or bring the grandchildren. He told me he was happy that I came and that I was his only friend. He said, 'Jesus must have sent you.' He talked to me about his wife and his dog. He said the days were long and there was nothing to do. I made him a picture of a black labrador, like his dog. He would cry and hug me."

Later, Jack shared his thoughts with Elisha, "Do you remember the first time you came? I scared you and was mean to you, but you still came back. I felt the world had left me and I wanted to die. I remember you touched my shoulder like you could feel my loneliness. And, when I looked into your eyes at that moment I decided I wanted to live. I've gone through hard times, but truly this is the toughest time. Before you came I just wanted to withdraw and escape from a life in which no one cared about me or wanted me. Many nights I would cry in bed. I just want to thank you."

Elisha recalls a day when she prayed with Jack and thanked God for their friendship. Tears were streaming from Jack's eyes as he told her that no one had ever prayed with him before. Elisha had never seen a grown man cry before, not even her own dad. She also remembers the time Jack shared a nightmare with her. In his dream he was kicked out of heaven. After hearing this, Elisha asked Jack if he knew for sure if he would go to heaven if he died. Jack said, "Oh, no, nobody knows that." Elisha knew it was time to share the gospel and she poured out all the love for God she had in her heart. Jack said that no one had ever shared those things with him before. He asked Jesus to come into his heart and be Lord of his life. He died two months later.

BRIDGE BUILDERS

Picture the Bridge Builders of Mechanicsville Christian Center ministering in a small Chicago city park. Downtown stores, dense crowds, and congested traffic surround the park. Forty-five children, with an average age of about 11, gather on the concrete stage area. One child prays, "Lord, show us where you are working in this city. Bring people to this park and save them." During this "heart prep" time, the children confess sins and ask God to show them His will for the outreach.

A child introduces "Sunday School Rock," a high energy, crowd-gathering song set to choreography. The music reverberates off the tall building and fills the intersection with sound. People stop and look in the direction of the park. Many draw closer to the stage – the homeless, men in business suits, cyclists, shoppers, and mothers with children.

The mood changes to intimate worship songs as the kids sing "All of My Heart" and "The Time Is Now." The pure, sincere relationship the children have with the Lord is so evident in their song and movement. It draws people, even mesmerizes them, as their looks turn into stares of amazement.

Cars slow down as they pass the park, and one car with a young couple with several small children stops in a traffic lane to watch and listen. Other cars honk and are forced to work their way around the obstruction.

After the songs, drama, and testimonies conclude, a teenager gives a salvation challenge. In teams of two or three, the children mingle with the crowd and minister to individuals, always under the watchful eye of the adult leaders. They ask, "Is there some way we can pray for you?" Almost everyone shares some need — a sickness, concern for their own children, or maybe a failing marriage. The innocent, sincere prayers of the kids seem to zing straight to the heart of God. The children even lead some people to Christ.

All around the park the Bridge Builders can be seen making a difference. A group of teenage boys are talking to a homeless man. A very shy girl, with an authority and anointing that is not her own, is explaining the gospel to an adult. Some 8-10 year old girls are sculpting balloons for a group of Hispanic children as they tell them about Jesus. Where are the adult leaders? They are the cheerleaders on the sidelines and the security at the perimeters. The children are doing it all. These kids have learned that they can make a difference. They don't even have to grow up first.

PREPARATION

For each of these children, the journey began six months earlier with a nine-page application on which they stated their reasons for wanting to join the Bridge Builders team. Attitude of the heart, not talent, determined who was selected. Team members began their preparation two months in advance by completing an age appropriate version of the "Experiencing

God," workbook by Henry Blackaby. This home study taught the children to recognize where God was working, and then how to join Him in that work.

Training was kicked into high gear with a one week "boot camp" before departing for Chicago. During boot camp the children followed a daily routine that included personal devotions, teaching, small group interaction, rehearsal of ministry skills, recreation, and corporate worship. The four to five hours of rehearsal each day focused on the development of three ministry skills: creative movement in worship, drama, and testimonies.

In Chicago the team lived in a host church and conducted two performing arts outreaches each day for a week in places like city parks, nursing homes, shopping malls, recreation programs, and even a fine arts festival.

"I HAVE GAINED HEART KNOWLEDGE"

Over the past 12 years, the Bridge Builders team has grown and now we have four summer teams instead of one. The children have made a difference in the communities where they have ministered, but the greatest difference I have seen is the change in their own hearts.

Hilary first joined the Bridge Builders team when she was 12 years old. She shares,

"Through going on outreach, I have fallen in love with Jesus. Instead of just gaining "head knowledge," I have gained "heart knowledge." Outreach has given me a chance to live out the things I learned in Sunday School, to really experience Jesus as Provider, Protector, Savior, Father, Peace, Lover, and so much more.

When we go on outreach, we put ourselves in a place where we are expecting and needing God to move. Instead of being complacent, we urgently seek Him — to provide finances, words to say, and directions for where we should go. When we seek

God, He shows up and each time He shows up, it causes me to love Him more. In Chicago, I remember faces: young, old, clean, dirty, sad, hateful, loving, kind. I remember the look in the eyes of someone that has never been held and loved as I tell them of God's undying love. I remember the joy and peace all over the faces of people who have just had their lives cleansed from sin and reconciled to God."

PRACTICAL SERVICE IN SOUTH CAROLINA

Community outreach is not limited to the performing arts. Gateway Christian Fellowship in Raleigh, North Carolina has an outreach team of kids called CrossWave. One summer these kids decided to minister to others through practical service. A Baptist church in South Carolina was one of many African-American churches burned down in the 90's by racially motivated arson. The CrossWave team joined the African-American and white community effort to rebuild the church. The kids cleaned many sooty areas, framed new walls for the bathrooms, cleaned and painted the vestibule, and placed insulation in the walls and ceiling of the sanctuary. The younger children built two picnic tables for the church grounds.

This was no easy project. Working conditions were hot and dirty. At times the kids felt so incapacitated all they could do was to lie on their sleeping bags and rest. Many prayed and trusted God for strength as they were stretched through demanding and unpleasant circumstances.

Throughout this outreach, God used the team to minister reconciliation, healing, and forgiveness among African Americans and whites. During one of their performing arts ministry times to the community, the team sang "We Will Stand."

You're my brother you're my sister,
So take me by the hand.
Together we will work 'till He comes.

There's no foe that can defeat us,
When we're walking side by side;
As long as we're together
We will stand.

REACHING THE COMMUNITY THROUGH SPORTS

Sports can also be a vehicle for community outreach. Tom Giglio, who was serving on the Executive Leadership Team of King's Kids International at the time of this story, ministered in the community through sports and practical service.

Tom brought one of his teams for an extended outreach into an inner-city neighborhood of Philadelphia. His team stayed in a small church that was located across the street from an inner-city park where neighborhood kids often played basketball. During the early part of the day, the team cleaned the park and painted over graffiti. Younger kids from the neighborhood began to gather around the team to see what was happening.

Later in the day the team played "pick up" basketball games with the kids in the neighborhood. Friendships between the team members and neighborhood kids developed. During the entire outreach, there was not one incident of team members losing their tempers. All the team members lived the Christian life before the neighborhood kids. Tom told me that when kids play ball like this, what's inside really comes out. The neighborhood kids could tell that these team members had a genuine relationship with Christ.

OPPORTUNITIES FOR OUTREACH
ARE UNLIMITED

This chapter could go on indefinitely with stories of kids making a difference in local communities across our nation. Children are ministering in shopping malls, hospitals, rehabilitation centers, hospices for the dying, homeless shelters, housing projects, community centers, and vacant lots. Kids are sorting items in food banks and ministering through clowning at county and state fairs. I even found a group of kids reaching the community through puppet shows on public access television.

Look at the people, resources and contacts that God has placed in your church. These will probably determine the type and location of your outreaches. Even an individual family can get started in community outreach. Just remember, although children are very effective in community outreach, our primary goal is to disciple our children in their faith. We are not "using" children to accomplish our personal outreach goals. Our priority is their safety and spiritual growth.

NEXT STEP READINGS

★ The "Mobilizing Kids for Outreach" manual and video by Pete Hohmann gives a step-by-step plan for involving children in community outreach. It covers topics like planning for an outreach, keeping children safe, and helping children process their experiences. The 25-minute video will show all the principles in action. You can order it by calling Gospel Publishing House at 1-800-641-4310 or 417-862-2781 ext 4009 (outside the US). It is order #715-204 and costs $30.00, which includes the manual and video. You can also log onto www.gph.org and type "mobilizing" into the search box. (Please note - "Mobilizing Kids for Outreach" is often listed as "Mobilizing Kids for Ministry").

★ Free handout from Pete Hohmann's "Conducting Community Outreach Where Kids Do The Ministry" workshop presented at the 2003 National Children's Pastors' Conference. Also available is an article published in the "Christian Education Counselor" magazine called "Investing Children in Mission." It features a snapshot of the Bridge Builders team ministering in Chicago. Request these at petehohmann@cs.com (sent as Microsoft Word attachments).

KIDS MAKING A DIFFERENCE IN THE WORLD

CRAIG KIELBURGER

A 12 year-old boy named Craig Kielburger reached for the comic section of the Toronto Star as he was getting ready for school. But, instead, a picture of a boy wearing a bright red vest with his fist held high on the front page caught his attention. The headline read, "Boy, 12, Murdered for Speaking Out Against Child Labor."

The article told the story of a young boy from Pakistan, Iqbal Masih, who was sold into child labor at the age of four and forced to work as a carpet weaver to pay back a six hundred rupee loan (less than $16) that his parents had made to pay for the wedding of their eldest son. Iqbal worked 12 hours a day, six days a week tying tiny knots to make carpets.

With the help of a human rights organization, Iqbal was able to escape and go back to school. By age 12, he became a powerful and eloquent speaker, gaining international attention as an uncompromising critic of child servitude. But, a few months after receiving the Reebok Human Rights Youth in Action Award in Boston, Iqbal was murdered in Pakistan.

HEARING WITH THE HEART

Craig had never heard about child labor and he didn't even

41

know where Pakistan was. But, the difference between his life and the lives of children who are forced into a life of slave labor shocked him. Because Craig read the article about Iqbal with his heart, and not just his head, he felt compelled to find out more about this problem. At the public library, he read articles about the 250 million child laborers in the world. That night, images filled his mind of children endlessly tying knots in carpets, working in mines, polishing gems, assembling matches and fireworks, and working in the sex trade. These reports so moved him, that he had difficulty focusing on his homework. Why was nothing being done to stop such cruelty?

Craig continued in his quest for information by contacting several humanitarian organizations. He discovered two things: first, that none of the organizations he contacted knew very much about child labor, and second, that no young people his age were involved in the child advocacy organizations he contacted.

A PROACTIVE GENERATION

Craig knew he had to do something. Craig is part of the Millennial Generation (kids born between 1982 and 2002). This generation can be characterized as "proactive." When faced with a problem they ask, "What are we going to do about it?" To make a difference, all this generation needs is some adults who stand by them and believe in them.

Craig asked permission from his 7th grade teacher to have a few minutes to speak to the students before class began. For a half-hour, Craig shared story after story about child labor, including the murder of Iqbal. Anger, sympathy and disbelief filled the room.

Craig then asked the class who would like to join a group that would look at what could be done to help these children. Eighteen hands shot up. That night, twelve of those students got together to prepare a display for a youth fair that was to be held later that week in the downtown area of Toronto. They only had two days to prepare. It would be a great first project that the newly formed group would tackle.

FREE THE CHILDREN

They still had no name for their group so they looked through news clippings for inspiration. One article reported a demonstration in Delhi, India, where 250 children had marched through the streets chanting, "We want education. We want freedom. Free the children!" "That's it!" someone shouted, and Free the Children was born.

Craig and his friends set up their "Free the Children" display at the youth fair in downtown Toronto. Right away, they noticed that the presenters at the fair were mostly adults who spoke about what their organizations were doing "for" children. Craig and his friends were the only children speaking for themselves. At that moment Craig realized that not only did children like Iqbal need to be freed from abusive labor, but children in his own culture needed to be freed from the misconception that they were not smart enough, old enough, or capable enough to contribute to social issues.

One of Craig's goals became letting kids know that they are capable of changing the world, they don't have to grow up first to make a difference. In addition to a letter writing campaign, the group also made presentations in local schools. They spoke to the city council of Toronto, which resulted in the passage of a resolution banning the purchase of fireworks made by children for any city event.

The following summer, Free the Children conducted a community garage sale. The children spent days washing, cleaning, painting, sorting and labeling the donated items. The garage sale included older kids dressed up as clowns, organized games, bead bracelet vendors, and a lemonade stand. The crowds grew, along with the traffic problems, and the TV news crews were right there to cover all the excitement.

A BIG BREAK FOR FREE THE CHILDREN

A big break came later that year. Craig was invited to speak to the 2,000 people attending the Ontario Federation of Labor Convention. Union members laughed as someone positioned a two-step stool for Craig to stand on so his head could be seen above the rostrum. He was scheduled for only three minutes and he could tell by the demeanor of those in charge that going over his time an extra second was not an option.

But Craig didn't sit down again until an hour and forty-five minutes later! After a 15-minute speech, he received standing ovations as labor union after labor union made pledges to Free the Children. In all, the 2,000 union members gave $150,000 to help build a rehabilitation and education center in Alwar, India. Additional lists of petition sheets had to be hurriedly photocopied to keep up with the crowds waiting to sign. The next day the Toronto Star printed the whole story on the front page.

SEEING THE PROBLEMS FIRST-HAND

A few weeks later, Craig was given an opportunity to go on a seven-week trip to Bangladesh, India and Pakistan with Alam Rahman, a recent university graduate who was born in Bangladesh. Alam became Craig's mentor and guide. While on this trip, Craig met with the Prime Minister of Canada, who happened to be in Asia for trade talks.

Seeing the poverty and abusive child labor firsthand had such a profound affect on Craig that he now divides his life into "pre-Asia" and "post-Asia." Everyone who is serious about helping kids become world-changers should read Craig's book, "Free the Children," which contains a well-written account of his trip.

FREE THE CHILDREN TODAY

Today, Free the Children has spread to more than 20 countries.

Their list of accomplishments includes raising funds to construct 20 schools in Latin America, assembling and shipping over 15,000 health care and school kits to children in poorer nations, digging of wells for safe drinking water, sending over $200,000 in medical supplies to Nicaragua, and starting several alternative income programs in India so kids can go back to school. Free the Children even purchased land and farming equipment for fatherless families in Nicaragua.

Through their petitions, Free the Children has played a major role in the introduction of new legislation designed to protect children. For example, after Craig met with the Minister of External Affairs in Ottawa, a new law was passed to allow Canada to prosecute citizens who travel abroad to molest children. Free the Children also played a role in the decision of Canadian rug merchants to support the "Rugmark" and "Fair Trade" labels. These labels certify that the carpets were not made with child labor. Free the Children also helped persuade the Brazilian government to spent an additional million dollars on programs to help child laborers.

Craig is also very involved in leadership training. Free the Children conducts in-school leadership training for grades 4-6, a Saturday leadership program called Youth Heroes, and summer leadership camps.

Maybe you are thinking that Free the Children must have become an "adult-run" organization in order to accomplish all these things. The opposite is true. Adults serve only as mentors and office workers. Policy decisions are only made by young people under 18 years-old. This is truly a "kid-run" organization.

TWO EXTREMES

In his book, "Free the Children," Craig talks about the two extremes in the world today regarding children. He writes:

"...I have found two extremes. In many developing countries,

children are often asked to work long hours at hazardous jobs with no opportunity to play or go to school. They are not allowed to develop physically, intellectually, and emotionally as they should. They support entire families. They fight in wars. They are given too much responsibility at too young an age.

On the other hand, in many industrialized countries everything is done for children. They are segregated most of their lives with the members of their own age group and are given little opportunity to assume responsibility, to develop a social conscience, or learn through interaction with adults. Through media they learn to be consumers, to gain their self-image through the electronic toys they own and the labels they wear. They, too, are exploited. They see violence and suffering on the news every day but are told that they are too young to do anything about it. They are conditioned to become passive bystanders. This is the other extreme. Marian Wright Edelman, founder of the Defense for Children International, once said, 'Affluenza' and lack of moral purpose are more dangerous viruses that influenza for millions of America's and the world's children."

CHILDREN ARE DREAMERS

Craig says that because children are dreamers, they are impossible to stop and because they are idealists, they always have faith in a better tomorrow. This statement and Craig's story reflect many of the characteristics of the Millennial Generation, which we will be discussing more in Chapter 7. It also shows that the great impact the Millennial Generation is making is not confined to a religious setting. Children are making a difference both within and outside the church.

TEN YEAR-OLD RAISES
OVER $5,000 FOR MISSIONS

Tyler VanBlarcom was only 10 years old when he decided

that kids can make a difference through giving to world missions. He attends First Assembly of God in Lake Wales, Florida.

In 2002, Tyler made a faith promise of $700 for BGMC (Boy's and Girl's Missionary Crusade). BGMC is a program that gives children in the Assemblies of God an opportunity to give to world missions. The money that is contributed by children help purchase needed resources such as Sunday School material for children in poorer countries. To make a faith promise, you ask God how much He wants you to give to missions, and then you believe that He will supply that money.

Tyler felt impressed in his heart that God wanted him to give a faith promise of $700 during the upcoming year, which is a lot of money for a 10 year-old. So, he prayed and asked God what he should do to earn money. Tyler began to share with his grandparents, aunt and uncle what BGMC is all about and how it helps missionaries. Tyler did odd jobs and chores and worked hard. He was driven by a desire for children like him around the world to learn about Jesus Christ.

By sharing his vision with his family members and working odd jobs, Tyler finished the year by giving $5,425.40 to BGMC! His contribution made up more than half the total amount that his church raised last year, $10,270.18.

CALLED TO MADAGASCAR

Craig was only 12 years-old when he decided to do something about the oppression of child labor. Justin Derting was only 7 when God called him to make a difference in Madagascar. A missionary to Madagascar named John Cunningham was speaking in Justin's church. John was showing slides to the congregation as he spoke. One slide in particular captivated seven-year old Justin. It was a picture of a homeless family sitting on the side of the street next to their cardboard box house. The kids were just playing around the cardboard houses. At that moment, Justin shares that God called him and said, "I need you to go talk to John Cunningham." He just started crying and his Dad asked him what was the matter. Justin told his dad that he needed to talk to the missionary and he did so after the service. John told Justin that he had been praying for somebody to come and help him in Madagascar.

After that Justin and John wrote letters back and forth. John would describe Madagascar and Justin would write back and ask questions. Finally, John wrote a letter asking if Justin's father could bring the family to Madagascar to serve on a 3-month work and witness team. They agreed, and Justin went on his first overseas missions trip at 10 years old. Justin was very interested in puppets, so this became the focus of their time in Madagascar. The Derting family equipped national workers to reach the street children with puppets.

A year later, the Derting family returned to Madagascar, this time for a year. They took John Cunningham's place while he was on furlough. Justin plans to attend Northwest Nazarene University and become a missionary when he grows up.

WHY MUST I HAVE EVERYTHING?

Jamie began ministering to others on the Bridge Builders team when she was 11 years old. At 13 she went with an adult team to Ecuador where she ministered in an orphanage and helped construct a Bible school. Her poem and other writings not only reveal her own developing missions world view, but also the heart for the world that God has placed within the Millennial Generation.

ME

Why must I have everything,
When they have nothing?
I laugh, smile, love, live.

They cry, scream, hate, fear.

Why must I have all I could ever want,
When they are always in need?
I'm fed, warm, loved, safe.
They're hungry, cold, alone, afraid.

Why must everything be easy for me,
When nothing is easy for them?
I want to hold them, hug them, love them, comfort them.
They're hit, beaten, bruised, scared.

Why can't I take some of the hurt off their shoulders,
When they have far too much to carry?
I have a home, money, food, hope.
They have streets, poverty, hunger, despair.

If only I could take the pain from their eyes and the defeat
from their footsteps...
But I only care about my needs.

If only I could take the cry from their souls and the
hopelessness from their voices...
But I am only concerned about my desires.

If only I could take the ache from their hearts and the hunger
from their spirits...
But I am only bothered with my wants.

If only I could take the sickness from their mind and the
hatred from their body...
But I only love myself.

It breaks my heart to see them hurt,
Yet I do nothing.

I cry for their souls,
Yet I do not move.

I have His never-ending love,
Yet I do not give it away.

O, God, forgive me,
And please Lord, help me love them.

Jamie writes,

"Lately, I've been spending a lot of time thinking of all I've been given. I've been so blessed. Too blessed, it seems. I have an incredible church, a loving family, supportive friends, and any material possession I could ever really need. At times, thinking about these things makes me feel so grateful, but at other times, I am overwhelmed with an incredible sense of guilt. Why have I been given so much when so many, too many, have nothing?"

"I think back to the faces I've seen on foreign shores. The faces of children — dirty, hungry, alone, abandoned. Children who roam the streets day after day. Children whose sole possessions are the scraps of clothing on their backs. Children who are so starved that they sniff glue in order to ignore the ache of their stomach. Their faces almost haunt me, mostly, because I know they are real. I've touched their hands, seen their tears, and kissed their faces. All awhile I am thinking, "Why God?" I know our God is just and fair, more than fair, so why then is the world like this? Why have I been given so much? Why haven't they? And then the answer comes, as it always does. It's the answer that comes from the throne room of God Himself. The answer that is not just for me, but for everyone."

"So you could go."

"When I ask these questions to my Father, He never says,

"Because I love you more." He doesn't. He never says, "Because you deserve it." I don't. He never says, "Because I messed up." He can't. The answer is always the same and always clear."

"So you could go."

"I've been given so much, too much, but only so that I can have so much to give. There is a responsibility that cannot be overlooked, ignored, or forgotten. I believe that God is saying that we have been blessed, not so we can just sit back and say, 'Thank you, Jesus,' but so that we can change our world."

"It still doesn't all make sense to me and there are so many things that I just don't understand, but I do know one thing. I can do something about it. Not because I am great or gifted or special, but because I serve a God who says, 'Go.' A God who promises to provide where He leads. A God whose heart aches for the lost. How often I say, 'Lord, I want to be like You,' but I am amazed how little I truly mean it. He gave all He had. Everything. For them. And I believe He is asking us to do the same."

"God, I pray that you would change me and equip me. Please give me the strength and courage to follow you . . . wherever You may lead."

Jamie is a few years older now. She is on the foreign missions committee at our church and is preparing for a full-time missions assignment in a foreign country. She has already completed a year of language training abroad.

Children are making a difference all around the world. It is through prayer like Hope Smith, through social activism like Craig, through raising money like Tyler VanBlarcom, or even going on missions trips like Justin and Jamie. Consider what you can do as a family. Or, consider how you can help the children in your church become involved in world missions.

NEXT STEP READINGS

✶ "Free the Children," by Craig Kielburger, HarperCollins Publishers

✶ www.21stcenturykidsconnect.org is a web site that lists missions resources for children and announces conferences that equip children's workers in missions education for children.

✶ Bob Sjogren's web site is www.jealousGOD.org and it has a section that lists missions resources for children. Enter the main screen (UnveilinGlory) and click on "Books" and then on "Kid's Only." Bob is an author, writer, international speaker, and missions mobilizer. He attends Mechanicsville Christian Center.

✶ www.4kids.ag.org is an Assemblies of God web site for children that has many stories about kids getting involved in missions.

✶ The "Mobilizing Kids for Outreach" manual and video by Pete Hohmann also contains several chapters on teaching missions to children. You can order it by calling Gospel Publishing House at 1-800-641-4310 or 417-862-2781 ext. 4009 (outside the US). It is order #715-204 and costs $30.00, which includes the manual and video. You can also log onto www.gph.org and type "mobilizing" into the search box. (Please note - "Mobilizing Kids for Outreach" is often listed as "Mobilizing Kids for Ministry").

✶ Free handout from Pete Hohmann's "Integrating Missions Into Sunday School and Children's Church" workshop presented at the 2003 National Children's Pastors' Conference. Request at petehohmann@cs.com (sent as a Microsoft World attachment).

7

THE MILLENNIAL GENERATION — GENERATION OF DESTINY

"He was no ordinary child" is the way that Acts 7:20 describes Moses. Likewise, the Millennial Generation is no ordinary generation. I believe they are a Generation of Destiny, planned by God to accomplish a great purpose. I believe they will be the generation that completes the Great Commission, bringing the gospel to every tongue, tribe and nation. I believe the Millennial Generation will usher in the return of the Lord Jesus Christ.

But, who are the Millennials and what are their characteristics? The answer to these questions will give us insight into God's purpose for them. Their characteristics are no accident, but have been planned by God since the beginning of the world.

WHO ARE THE MILLENNIALS?

We have defined the Millennial Generation as those children born between 1982 and 2002. Most of us reading this book are probably Boomers (born 1943 to 1960) or Generation X (born 1961 to 1981). If you are a Boomer you tended to be more self-indulgent with a greater inward focus. You came of age during the consciousness awakening of the 60's and 70's. If you are a member of Generation X, you grew up in a time when youth tended to be under-protected and criticized for their risk-taking behaviors. You may have felt somewhat

alienated from society.

Then, along comes the Millennials. This is their preferred name, but they are also known by other names such as Generation Y, Generation Next, Digital Generation, Net Generation, Y2 Kids, Generation Tech, and Generation.com.

SECULAR RESEARCH ON MILLENNIALS

The book, "Millennials Rising: The Next Great Generation," by Howe & Strauss, is a comprehensive analysis of the Millennial Generation. It is based on empirical data collected through valid and reliable polls conducted by the authors. It is a secular book, not a promotion of any religious agenda or ideal. The following are a few of the characteristics of the Millennials that the book lists:

∗ Millennials experience more pressures and higher expectations from parents than the previous generation.

∗ They have a stronger sense of family values, although their families are more diverse than traditional families of the past.

∗ They are remarkably upbeat about the future and about their generation's ability to make a difference and bring about change.

∗ They are relational team players. They figure out a solution, organize, share burdens, and get the job done in a way that often stuns adults. They believe they can overcome any obstacle if they just work together.

∗ They are pro-active and civic-minded. Millennials are committed to changing the world. When confronted with a problem they ask, "What can we do about it?"

∗ They are very interested in the supernatural. They believe in almost any expression of a higher being or higher power. They seek direct spiritual experiences and are not content to just hear about them.

"IF THEY CAN'T...WE WILL"

Remember our opening story about Barb Vogel's 4th grade class redeeming slaves in Sudan? "Millennials Rising" also sites this story in a quote by Robert Hoffman. He says, "A group of 4th and 5th graders in Aurora, Colorado...decided to collect money to buy back slaves in the Sudan. One of the children said, 'What are we going to do about this?' Unimaginable 15 years ago. Boomers would have gotten high and contemplated it. Xers would have written angst-filled songs about it. The Millennials, only 10 years old, are doing something about it. When asked why the 'leaders' aren't doing anything, a child replied, 'If they can't...we will.'"

A quote in "Millennials Rising" by Vincent Schiraldi, Justice Policy Institute, says, "We like to let people in on a little secret. These kids [Millennials] are less likely to take drugs, less likely to assault somebody else, less likely to get pregnant and more likely to believe in God."

POWER RANGER KIDS

In a workshop presented at the National Children's Pastors' Conference, Sharon Ellard, who is a children's consultant for the Assemblies of God, shared that some clues to the Millennial Generation can be found in the television shows they watch. Power Rangers, for example, were idolized by kids in the 90's and are still watched today. But, how does a show like this reflect the Millennials? Like the Power Rangers, the Millennials believe that they can magically transform themselves into a massive force against evil by simply working together. In fact, they prefer to work in teams rather than work by themselves.

I believe this is part of the reason that our Bridge Builders team has had such phenomenal success these past ten years. This intergenerational outreach team has provided the children of our church with a means to advance God's Kingdom through working together. But, unlike the Power Rangers, the evil they are overcoming is real. And, it is not a magic that empowers them, but the real power of God's Spirit.

MILLENNIALS LIKE TO PARTNER WITH ADULTS

Millennials like to volunteer alongside adults. This is different, however, than just following adult leaders. They want to partner with adult workers in ministry. Hilary, who started ministering through Bridge Builders at age 12, states it this way: "In Bridge Builders, ownership of the team is given to the children. They are encouraged to pray about decisions that are made and to give their opinions. This is a ministry team for children, by children. The kids are not just told what they are going to do for God, but they are able to have input into how they will serve Him. One of the ways this is done is the older children are given the opportunity to participate in leadership positions."

This is a big paradigm shift for many children's workers who are used to occupying the center stage of ministry. As adults, however, we must be willing to function more like facilitators and equippers, and less as the experts who direct all the ministry.

MILLENNIALS ARE SENSITIVE
TO THE SUPERNATURAL

Millennials have a tremendous appetite for spiritual things. They sense something real in the spiritual world. They seem to have an increased sensitivity to the promptings of the Holy Spirit. When equipped, they are more likely than adults to have impressions or pictures in their heart from God during times of prayer or worship.

For example, Michael, age 11, shared a picture God gave him during a Bridge Builders summer outreach. Our theme that summer was "Anointed to Serve." Anointing is simply power from the Holy Spirit to serve God. During a time of worship, Michael saw in his mind a large, transparent, hollow statue of a man. He then saw anointing oil coming down and filling the statue. What was unusual, however, was that the statue was being filled in the head first as if the laws of gravity had been suspended.

Michael felt that this showed the anointing would be a work of God, not something natural. He also noted that there were barriers that occasionally hindered the oil from filling the statue completely. The barriers, he shared, represented sins in our life, but as the barriers were surrendered to the Lord and we asked forgiveness of sins, the obstacles were removed and the oil continued flowing.

This picture became a reminder of the importance of God's anointing during the outreaches. It reminded the kids that God would not give them power to serve and witness if they had sin in their hearts such as bad attitudes. All this would have been lost, however, if the leaders had failed to recognize the spiritual sensitivity of kids today. The simple question, "What is God showing you?" enabled the Holy Spirit to move through a child and touch many lives.

THE MILLENNIALS ARE READY
TO BE RADICALLY CHALLENGED

Joyce Satter, who was a national leader for King's Kids International, sums up the characteristics of the Millennials in an unpublished manuscript. "Millennials don't believe science has all the answers for their problems. They are open to spiritual solutions. The Millennials are a ripe generation, ready for challenge. They don't want to be entertained, but radically challenged. They want to know that they can make a difference. They are looking for destiny and purpose. They want someone to show them who they are. They want to find something worth living for, and even dying for. Like today's adults, they know they have a responsibility to change their world. But unlike our generation, they don't want to wait until they are adults to do it."

DESCRIBING THEMSELVES

But, how do the children, themselves, describe their generation? Step into a combined third through fifth grade Sunday School class at my church. The partitions that normally separate these three grades have been pulled aside for the last 15 minutes of Sunday School. I ask the children, "Do you feel your generation is special?"

Some of their responses reflect personal hopes and dreams. Daniel, age 10, shares, "I think our generation will bring more people to Christ. I think God is going to use me for a preacher. I always have wanted to lead people to Christ." Ben, age 10, adds, "I think that most of the children will share the Word all around the world. I think I will bring up [start] my own church."

A common theme among the responses of the children is the completion of the Great Commission. Logan, age 10, shares, "I believe my generation will spread the Word to the far reaches of the world. That way, before Jesus returns, everyone would have had a chance to know Christ." Ben, age 11, echoes the same thought, but adds that kids don't have to grow up first. "I feel that this generation of kids will be the generation that tells the whole world that Jesus loves them. I believe that kids right now can tell the world about God."

Technology is seen as an important ingredient for completing the Great Commission. William, age 9, shares, "I think we will be able to use new stuff to take the gospel all over the nation and maybe all over the world." Kerith, age 11, comfortably blends technology and spirituality together. "Our generation is special because we are individuals that can change the world. With faith, hope, love, God, and new technology, we can help others. We are different and the words we say can bring peace and happiness."

The possibility of Christ returning during their lifetime is not a fear, but rather a hope for most of the children. Emily, age 7, shares, "I hope my generation will be here when Jesus comes back." Jesse, age 11, agrees. "I think that my generation is going to reach kids dramatically because I think these are the last days." Jessica, age 11, adds, "I feel honored because most of the people who have passed away will not see the Lord in their lifetime. We may see the Lord in our lifetime." Rachel, age 10, confidently states, "I feel my generation will be here when Jesus comes back."

AN ACCIDENT OR GOD'S DESIGN?

What a wonderful generation! One day as I was pondering all these characteristics, it became so clear to me that the Millennial Generation is uniquely designed to complete the Great Commission and usher in the return of Christ. Of course, we don't know for certain when these events will occur, but it certainly seems that the Millennial Generation will play an important role in the history of the world.

The children who lived in Moses' day also played an important role in the history of the world. This generation would take possession of the Promised Land. The nation of Israel would be built upon this generation and the Law would be given to them. The generation of children when Jesus was born was also a key generation. They would grow up to establish the Christian church thirty years later.

GENERATIONS UNDER ATTACK

As we look at the Moses generation and the Jesus generation, we also see that they came under special attack. The Pharaoh over Egypt in Moses day tried to destroy the Hebrew children by having them killed at birth (Exodus 1:16). It seems that

Satan's intent was to prevent a child with a special destiny from growing to maturity and accomplishing God's purpose. Satan perceived that God was sending a deliverer who would threaten his kingdom. He tried to thwart God's plan.

Likewise, King Herod tried to kill the boys who were two years old or younger in Jesus' day (Matthew 2:16). Today is no different. Once more, a generation of destiny, perhaps the last and most important generation to ever live, is under attack. Through violence, abortion, slave labor, AIDS, homelessness, war, and sexual exploitation, millions of children around the world today are being brutally attacked by the enemy.

CHILDREN IN CRISIS

While it's true that America has entered a pro-child era, children around the world are suffering as never before. One of my first writing assignments was to contribute a chapter to a book called, "Children in Crisis," which was edited by Phyllis Kilbourn (MARC). This book highlights the problems that children around the world face today.

✶ Malnutrition: 35,000 children die of malnutrition every day (World Vision)

✶ Abortion: Every year, 40 million children lose their lives through parental consent. (UN documents)

✶ Family disintegration and abandonment: There are at least 160 million children who live or work on the streets of our cities. (UNICEF)

✶ Sex Exploitation, rape and abuse: There are at least 10 million children currently suffering the oppression of forced prostitution, and another million join this industry each year. (World Vision)

✶ War: From 1984-1994, 1.5 million children were killed in wars, over 4 million were disabled and blinded and 12 million lost their homes. Over 35 nations have

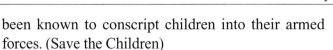

been known to conscript children into their armed forces. (Save the Children)

✶ Slavery and Abusive Child Labor: Over 100 million children are currently involved in child labor. (UN Children's Fund)

✶ Today's children face a level of psychological pressure totally unknown to previous generations. Faced with unattainable goals and a culture with few answers, many see suicide as the logical way out. (I believe we are seeing this today in the wave of young suicide bombers - Pete).

ROBBING KIDS OF TRUE PURPOSE

But, as fierce as this frontal assault seems, Satan has an even more insidious means of destroying the Millennial generation. It is not so obvious, but it is actually more effective. He robs kids of true purpose. In fact, he not only robs them of true purpose, but he replaces true purpose with a counterfeit purpose — self-gratification. He gets kids to believe that there is no greater purpose than themselves. But self-gratification is really no purpose at all, and it only leaves kids disillusioned and without hope.

DESIGNED FOR TRUE PURPOSE

But, what is true purpose? What is the purpose worth living for? I believe Genesis 12:1-3 gives us the answer. It says that God wants to bless us and make us a blessing to ALL the nations. Within this Scripture we see a top line blessing and a bottom line responsibility.

God wants to bless us. He wants us to enjoy an intimate relationship with Him. We were created to worship God and fellowship with Him. But, God also wants us to be a blessing to all the nations, to establish a church among every tongue, tribe and nation. This is our bottom line responsibility.

Together this top line blessing and bottom line responsibility form God's two-fold purpose throughout the Bible. This is the purpose that I believe the Millennials were designed to fulfill. They hunger to experience God directly. They have a tremendous capacity to love God. And, God placed deep within their hearts a desire to make a difference in the lives of others around the world.

There are children like Craig Kielburger and Hope Smith all around us. Groups of kids like Barb Vogel's 4th graders are just waiting for adults to stand with them. Many have even compared the Millennial generation to the Hero generation of World War II that liberated the world from oppression. But, will the children in your family or sphere of influence realize their destiny? The next and last chapter will focus on you, the most strategic generation I believe has ever lived.

NEXT STEP READINGS

✶ "Millennials Rising: The Next Great Generation," Howe & Strauss, Vintage Books. I think this is a "must read" for anyone who works with children today and who wants to understand the Millennial Generation.

✶ "Children in Crisis," Phyllis Kilbourn, MARC

✶ Free handout from Pete Hohmann's "Generation of Destiny" workshop presented at the 2003 National Children's Pastors' Conference. Request at petehohmann@cs.com (sent as a Microsoft Word attachment).

THE STRATEGIC GENERATION
— THE EQUIPPERS

If the Millennials truly are a Generation of Destiny, then what does that make us, the Boomers and the Gen Xers? I believe that we, the parents and children's workers, are a STRATEGIC generation, because it is our responsibility to equip the Millennials to fulfill their purpose.

UNDERSTANDING THE TIMES

Hidden in the genealogies in the book of First Chronicles in the Old Testament is an interesting comment on the tribe of Issachar. It says, "…the men of Issachar, who understood the times and knew what Israel should do…." Unlike the other tribes who were noted for their experienced soldiers, Issachar was noted for its discerning men who understood the times and knew what Israel should do.

In the last chapter, we saw how the generations of children that lived in the time of Moses and Jesus came under special attack. We also see how the parents of both Moses and Jesus "understood the times and knew what they should do."

Moses' parents took drastic action to save their child. Hebrews 11:23 says, "By faith Moses' parents hid him for three months after he was born, because they saw he was no ordinary child, and they were not afraid of the king's edict." Moses parents were willing to take radical action to fulfill the

destiny of their child.

Matthew 2:13-14 records, "…an angel of the Lord appeared to Joseph in a dream. 'Get up,' he said, 'take the child and his mother and escape to Egypt. Stay there until I tell you, for Herod is going to search for the child to kill him.' So he got up, took the child and his mother during the night and left Egypt…." Once again, we see parents taking drastic action to save their child. Both these sets of parents understood the times and they knew what they should do.

Parents, children's workers, and pastors must understand the times and know what they should do in order to prepare the Millennial Generation for their destiny. Only God the Father knows when Christ will return, but it is clear that the Millennials have a unique purpose in the plans of God. They are a new generation that will require new approaches to prepare them to fulfill their God-designed purpose.

Setting an example for us, the parents of Moses and Jesus discerned the times and knew what they should do to prepare their child for his special destiny. But in their stories, we also see that there was a critical window where they needed to obey God and respond. At just the right time Moses' parents placed him in the river at a location where Pharaoh's daughter would discover him. At just the right time Jesus' parents fled to Egypt. In both of these cases, to miss this critical window would have been catastrophic. But, are there also critical windows in the lives of our own children?

CRITICAL WINDOWS

Although every year of a child's life is important, there are two important windows that I would consider "critical." The first window is the preschool years. During the preschool years most attitude formation occurs. These attitudes include how a child feels about God, the church, and authority. As a professional counselor, I can tell you that these attitudes are extremely difficult to change once they have been established.

Therefore, relationships are critical with preschoolers, even more important than the cognitive facts they are taught. Preschool children's workers are actually modeling God, the church, and authority. Therefore, the nursery and preschool ministries in our churches should be a priority, not just a place to warehouse children while the adults do church together.

The worker-to-child ratio in preschool ministries should be low (a worker to every five children) and the children should always see a familiar face (our preschool directors are in the classroom every week, whereas our workers may only serve once a month). Needless to say, workers need to lavish love on preschool children and interact with them often on a one-to-one basis.

The preteen years (ages 10-12) are our second critical window. Those who have raised or taught preteens know that these kids dwell in the "in between age." They are no longer little children, but not quite teenagers.

You probably noticed that the flannel graph stories and secret code word searches in Sunday School just don't seem to have the same impact as they did with the younger children. In fact, many of this age group have grown bored with Christianity and are just going through the motions of memorizing material, only to quickly forget it the following week.

THEORETICAL KNOWLEDGE
WITHOUT PROVEN KNOWLEDGE

Because of this boredom with Christianity, many are lost at this age, even though their parents may faithfully bring them to church each Sunday. Why does this happen? Could it be that there has been an accumulation of theoretical knowledge in their minds, but not a proven knowledge of God? In other words, could it be that they are bored with their Christianity because they have not been given opportunities to personally prove that the promises of God are true? Their ideas and beliefs remain untested, and therefore are not integrated into their own faith in a meaningful way.

PROVIDE OPPORTUNITIES TO MINISTRY

There is no better place for children to prove God's Word is true and test their ideas and beliefs than through ministering to others. When children are given opportunities to minister to others, they find themselves in situations where they must depend on God. And, God is faithful to prove His Word true to them. Faulty ideas and beliefs are discarded and are replaced by the proven Word of God. Children become excited about their faith as they come to know God through experience.

This has been true for all generations, but I believe this is especially true for the Millennial Generation. They are designed to make a difference. They are proactive and want to minister alongside adults. They want to work together as a team to accomplish God's purposes. Children of all ages in the Millennial Generation want to make a difference, but it is CRITICAL that PRETEEN Millennials be given opportunities to minister to others.

GOD PROVES HIMSELF FAITHFUL TO CHILDREN

Let me give you a simple example of how children acquire a proven knowledge of God and an excitement about their faith through ministering to others. One summer, our children were scheduled to do an outreach at a drug rehabilitation center. Normally, an outreach consisted of an hour of singing with choreography, drama, and testimonies. After this, groups of two or three children would pray with the people who came to listen.

Usually, a small advance team would arrive an hour early at the ministry site with sound equipment so that it could be set up and ready when the kids arrived. Well, the kids arrived but the van with the sound equipment was lost and was almost an hour late. We also left the backup tapes and emergency boom box in the advance team van accidentally.

Minutes before the outreach was scheduled to begin, one of the children said, "We need to pray." Of their own initiative, they gathered in a circle and began to pray for the missing van. After several of the children prayed, one of the children ended the prayer time and said "Amen." At the exact moment the "Amen" was sounded, the van turned up the driveway of the rehabilitation center. The sound system was quickly set up and the response of the people was overwhelming. Most of the children commented that it was the best outreach of the summer.

A small miracle? Maybe a coincidence? Or, perhaps it was God proving to the kids that His Word is true. I'm sure we've all heard of more world-impacting miracles than this, but with each "small miracle," a child gains a proven knowledge of the Word instead of just a theoretical knowledge. Did I tell you how excited the kids were when the van appeared? They went crazy! In a similar way, kids who are given an opportunity to experience the faithfulness of God are excited about their faith. There is no better way to provide these opportunities to experience God's faithfulness than through equipping children to minister to others.

MAKING THE TRANSITION FROM
JUST RECEIVING TO GIVING

All mature believers who are excited about their Christianity have somewhere made the transition from just receiving ministry to actively ministering to others. As we have seen, a critical window where this transition needs to occur is the preteen years. Unless a preteen is given opportunities to minister to others, boredom with Christianity will often set in.

Some youth pastors, however, feel that if kids can just be delivered to them in their high school years, they can equip them for ministry through something like a missions project to Mexico. But, the reality is that many kids are lost before they even make it to high school youth group age. Like the lost window of opportunity for developing right attitudes in early elementary kids, another window of opportunity is often lost with the preteens when we fail to equip them to minister to others.

A TRIBAL GOD

When we fail to equip children to minister to others, what God are we giving them? At the first International Children's Expo, keynote speaker Jan Bell, stated that church workers often view children as the object of their ministry, rather than equipping them to *do* the work of ministry. Much of the message given to children helps them feel good about themselves: "God loves me and cares for me; Jesus will help me in times of trouble." These truths are important, but God's purpose for humanity does not stop there.

Bell warns that this me-centered concept can give children the perception of a "tribal god" who works for them alone and who has power limited to their circumstances. Such a narrow view of God leaves little motivation to reach out to others.

Once again, equipping children to minister to others will help them be more "other-centered" instead of "me-centered." Discipling them to minister to others will impart to them a purpose greater than themselves.

GOD HAS BECOME REAL TO ME

Ministering to others has impacted my daughter, Hannah. Being raised as an MK (missionary kid) and PK (pastor's kid) is not always easy. There is a tendency for PK's and MK's to be somewhat bored with their Christianity, and my daughter was probably no exception. But, providing opportunities for my daughter to minister in the community created an excitement in her about her faith. She explains this in her own words.

"When I was 10, I got involved in Bridge Builders, which is a kid's ministry team and I've been doing it for about six years. I've felt the presence of God, and I know the effect He has on my life. God has become real to me. He is no longer a story I was told as a child, but He is real and true. I really believe that is the problem so many teenagers have. They haven't found God to be real. I guess God showed me this when I was in New York. I was talking to a homeless man who had absolutely nothing. I handed him a sandwich and a blanket and I saw the joy pour through his soul. He found the love of God in that (what I thought to be gross) sandwich. There I felt the true love of God, too. God has become my father and my friend. At times when I really don't want to go on, He always does something to reveal himself to me. God has given me a vision for the lost. He seems to place people in my life that need him desperately."

CHRIST DIED TO RAISE UP
EXTRAORDINARY KIDS

In his book, "Equipping the Younger Saints," David Walters states, "Jesus did not pay the terrible price of dying on the cross to have a church full of bored apathetic kids. His plan is not to raise up a bunch of ordinary kids like the ones in the world. He died and rose again to raise up extraordinary kids." Furthermore, he shares, "God is bringing about a fresh vision today, showing parents and children's teachers how to equip children to be mighty for God. I don't believe kids can be mighty for God unless we have a vision for their spiritual capacity and equip and release them to ministry."

SEEING THEIR SPIRITUAL CAPACITY

Without a vision for the spiritual capacity of our children we will hinder them from developing into their full potential. You might say, "I would never hinder a child!" But, let me ask you the following questions:

* Have you ever acted as though you were spiritually superior to children?

* Was there a time when you really didn't listen to what a child was saying because you didn't believe that God could speak through a child?

* Did you ever harbor attitudes of unbelief concerning the spirituality of children?

* Did you ever belittle children and wound their spirit?

* Did you ever exclude children from participating in spiritual activities with adults?

* Were you ever overprotective, not allowing a child to minister to others for fear they would not be successful?

I think we all need to plead guilty to at least one of the above. But when we consistently treat children in these ways they will begin to feel that their spirituality is not valued. While it is true that a child will probably not pastor a church or even teach a Sunday School class, we need to see that they are equally important in the Kingdom of God. Here is the key: Different responsibilities but equal importance.

I think most of us would agree that the Holy Spirit indwells the believer upon conversion, regardless of your denominational background. The Holy Spirit regenerates our spirit upon repentance and is the life of God within us. But what Holy Spirit do children receive? A baby Holy Spirit? A junior Holy Spirit? No! Children receive the same Holy Spirit as adults. Therefore the Holy Spirit can speak to children and empower them to minister to others.

ELI'S EXAMPLE

First Samuel 3 speaks to us about the importance of recognizing the spiritual capacity of our children. First Samuel 1 records how Hannah made a vow to the Lord when she realized she was barren. She told the Lord that if she had a child, she would dedicate him to the Lord to serve in the temple all his life. Hannah conceived, named the child Samuel, and when he was weaned, she kept her vow and delivered Samuel to the high priest, Eli.

One night in the Temple, the Lord called Samuel, but he was still a very young boy and he did not know how to respond to the voice of the Lord. It was Eli who recognized the spiritual capacity of Samuel and instructed him how to respond to God. Samuel went on to be a leader of the nation, even while he was still a child.

Although Eli was not a great father in many ways, we need to follow his example regarding how he recognized the spiritual capacity of Samuel and equipped him to be a prophet of Israel. Eli recognized that Samuel could hear from God and obey Him. He believed that Samuel could minister to others, even when he was still a child.

Our children have great spiritual capacity. They can bring joy to God's heart. They can hear and obey God. They can minister to others. But, they are totally dependent on us to equip them to do these things.

PRAYING FOR OUR CHILDREN

We also need to follow Hannah's example in her dedication of Samuel to the Lord (First Samuel 1). As parents, we should pray, "Lord, accomplish your greatest purposes through my child. I dedicate and release my child to you." We can trust God with our children, just as Hannah trusted God with Samuel. God loves our children far more than we do and there is no better or safer place for our children to be than in the center of God's will.

Like Hannah's vow, I believe this above prayer goes beyond the simple prayer of petition — our prayer must be a faith declaration. By faith we daily declare that God's greatest purposes will be accomplished in our children. Every time fear creeps into our hearts concerning our children, we should declare God's ability to shape our children into world changers. Because we are parents, I believe we have been given the privilege to pray in this manner for our children in a way that no one else can.

AFFIRMATION

I am sure that Eli and Hannah affirmed young Samuel. Affirmation is second only to prayer. We probably all affirm our children, but what are we affirming? This is a critical question because a child will grow into the things that we affirm. For example, if we lavish our greatest affirmation on our children for physical beauty, athletic ability, or grades in school, our children will come to value these things above all else. But, if we affirm virtues like compassion for the hurting and concern for the lost, we will be shaping our children to fulfill God's greatest purposes in their lives.

TAKING A RISK

Unfortunately, many of us fail to follow the model of Hannah and Eli in the Old Testament, or even the example set for us by the parents of Hope, Monica or Craig. In our desire to protect children from being pushed out of their comfort zones, we may actually be "protecting" them from God's greatest purpose for their lives. Children need "classroom of life' experiences that usually only occur as they move out of their comfort zones and minister to others.

This doesn't mean that we push our children into uncomfortable situations and then let them fend for themselves. No! We prepare them to minister to others through training and equipping. This preparation is just another word for discipleship.

Next we then support them as they minister to others. Our goal is to maximize their success. We are like mentors, facilitators and cheerleaders on the sidelines. We release ministry to them while always supporting them.

Finally we help children process their experiences. Anything worth doing is worth debriefing. We ask them questions like, "What did you learn?" "How did you experience God?" "How did God use you?" The teachable moments that arise from debriefing become the building blocks of character.

STANDING WITH CHILDREN

I am still deeply moved when I read the incredible stories of children like Hope, Monica, Craig, or Barb's 4th grade class. But, what is the common thread that binds all these world changers together? In each case, there was an adult, usually a parent, who stood by them.

Hope's mom imparted a belief in prayer and a concern for Mongolia to her daughter. Monica's parents opened their home for a Bible study to disciple the people that their daughter led to the Lord. Barb Vogel enlarged the worldview of her students through opening their eyes to slavery in Sudan. And, when Craig Kielburger was only 13 years old, his parents released him to go on a 7-week tour of Asia to observe first-hand the abuses of child labor.

If an adult had not stood with these children, they probably would not have impacted the world in the ways we have seen. The Millennial Generation has a tremendous capacity to make a difference in the world, they have been uniquely designed by God for a special purpose. But they are still dependent on us, as adults, to equip them for that purpose.

As parents and children's workers, we need to believe in our children and stand with them. We must equip them for ministry instead of just making them the object of our ministry. We must impart a purpose to kids that is greater than themselves. Kids must be taught that they can make a difference right now. They don't have to grow up first.

PICK A PLACE TO START

Right now, right here, pick a place to start. Whether you are a parent, a Sunday School teacher, or even a children's pastor, how can you provide opportunities for your children to make a difference? How can they be equipped and released to minister to others? Hopefully a story in this book has provoked the thought, "My kids could do that!"

May God use you to equip and mobilize the children He has placed in your sphere of influence, whether they be your own children or children in your church. I believe there is nothing more strategic you can do for the Kingdom of God.

NEXT STEP READINGS

✴ Free handout from Pete Hohmann's "Equipping Kids for Ministry" workshop presented at the 2003 National Children's Pastors' Conference. Request at petehohmann@cs.com (sent as a Microsoft Word attachment)

✴ Consider going to a National Children's Pastors' Conference sponsored by the International Network of Children's Ministry (not just for pastors). Get more information at www.incm.org or call 1-800-324-4543.

ORDERING COPIES

Additional copies of "Kids Making A Difference" can be ordered by emailing petehohmann@cs.com or calling Mechanicsville Christian Center at 804-746-4303 and asking for Pastor Pete. Or, you can send a check for **$9.00** ($7.00 for the book plus $2.00 postage) to:

Pete Hohmann
Mechanicsville Christian Center
8061 Shady Grove Road
Mechanicsville, VA 23111

Address checks to "Pete Hohmann." Discounts are available for larger orders. The writing and printing of "Kids Making A Difference" is a personal, non-profit venture. My only goal is to mobilize the Millennial Generation. In no way I am financially profiting from the stories of the children in this book.